(It's **NOT** OK to NOT be OK)

'I will never attend an anti-war rally; if you have a Pro -peace rally, invite me."

Mother Teresa

The Mindset Movement Mission

To the fans and readers of this book, who are dedicated to changing their own world and the world of others for the better. You are invited to join our community; we are inviting you to be a part of the change.

Visit us at – www.mindset-movement.co.uk

It is our mission, to positively impact as many lives as possible, one day at a time.

By flooding our brains with positivity, sharing our success stories, discussing our difficulties, challenges, and experiences, and most importantly sharing how we overcome them. We will show anyone who might be in their own hour of need, who might be needing that little bit of inspiration to change their own mindset, that it is possible.

Together we can change, not only our own mindset but that of our future generations.

Intro

In the new thought philosophy, the Law of Attraction is a pseudoscience. It is based on the belief that positive or negative thoughts bring positive or negative experiences into a person's life. The Law of Attraction dictates that whatever can be imagined and held in the mind's eye is achievable if you take action on a plan to get to where you want to be. The theory is that the energy of our thoughts (positive or negative) attracts experiences of the same energy to come into our lives. The concept is generally summed up as "Like attracts like."

"Create the highest, grandest vision possible for your life,

because you become what you believe."

Oprah Winfrey

"It's okay to not be okay".

This saying has never sat well with me because, NO actually, it is not okay, to not be okay! Why are we saying that? I don't know about you, but I want all my loved ones, as well as myself to be "OKAY".

I am "Pro OKAY".... Pro abundance, pro wealth, pro health, pro life, pro love, pro peace, pro harmony, pro unity!

We are in a world where we are putting so much focus on mental health issues yet suicide rates, especially in men are rising at an alarming rate. Something clearly isn't working!

It seems that having a bad day these days qualifies as having a mental health issue! Anxiety, stress, and depression, all very real and serious diagnosis are being thrown about like never before and its sad, really sad to hear (literally) so many young people, comparing over lunch who has the worst case of anxiety and what anti-depressants each of them is on. Sharing how terrible their life is and generally just engaging in thoroughly negative conversation.

I'm not saying we shouldn't feel ok about talking about mental health and our feelings, but I truly believe that we have become so focused and consumed on negative thoughts, that it is damaging us.

In one of the many books, I have read and believe to be true, it talks about the science of suggestion. The power of suggestion is huge. It talks about how we can literally, make a person ill by constantly suggesting to them that they don't look well.

If this is the case, shouldn't we be focusing on and encouraging the recognition of the positive "goings on" in our lives? Instead, we seem to constantly be encouraging people to talk about and focus on how terrible everything is. And, it's all around us everywhere we look. We see it on the news, in magazines, in the papers, social media. We are always fighting something! The fight against cancer, the fight against racism, the fight against illegal immigration, the fight against terrorists. The words we use, the words we hear and read are fundamental to how we perceive the world and how our bodies react and respond.

Did you know, the word "Fight", especially repeated over and over can actually create a chemical reaction in our brains?

Every time we have or prompt a negative thought, we flood our brains with cortisol (the "neggy" chemical) whilst it does have its uses, it is the opposite to dopamine (the "happy" chemical). Whatever we flood our brains with the most becomes our brains "preferred drug" and so behind the scenes our brains work harder and harder to obtain more of it.

Scientific studies show that most of us have more negative thoughts in a day, than positive ones. So, we are essentially flooding our brains with cortisol, and our brains love it. We are addicted to being negative and we can't seem to stop feeding that addiction. We are being conned by our addict little brains to supply it with a drug that actually makes us feel miserable, and we go looking for more of it at every opportunity.

Sound familiar? You know that person who only seems to be happy when there is a problem to focus on and complain about, I know a few. Hell, I became one!

The good news is it doesn't have to be this way. Standing by, ready and waiting is dopamine the happy drug. All we must do is tip the balance. If we flood our brains with this "happy drug" our brains will then prefer that as its natural state and will go after seeking "happy". I find this fascinating; it blows my druggy little mind!

So, now the science lesson is over, don't you agree that we should be preparing our younger generation in how they can take the reins of their own minds and control this? Should we not, be preparing them for the fast paced, competitive, sometimes damn right difficult days ahead? Should we not, be focussed on preparing them that they won't always come first, they won't always be right, that life isn't always fair and that they won't always win. That they won't get a medal for coming 6th place because the real world, just isn't like that.

Our kids today, come of age, go out to the real world and BAM! They haven't been given the tools to deal with what faces them and they crumble. Life can be tough, and they just aren't prepared for it. We ask ourselves often, what's happened to the youth of today, why suicide rates are up, why is my child struggling with this, why am I struggling with this. Why me, why my child, why, why, why. The hard truth is, it's us! We have allowed this to happen! Not only to them but to ourselves.

We teach them that you get rewarded with a shiny little medal for coming 6th place in a race, yet we appear dumbstruck when they aren't willing to put any effort in to achieving anything of any real use. We have allowed social media to convince them that they aren't pretty or that they are overweight, we allow them to believe that the contestants on all of these reality TV shows are who we should be aspiring to. That being chosen by the "hunky guy" based on looks alone is how the world works and that it is Okay. Many of us have even become convinced of this ourselves. We teach them and tell ourselves "It's okay to not be okay" and prescribe anti-depressants like we are handing out candy, at Halloween. I'm aware of kids as young as 16 years old, who have been diagnosed with depression and have been prescribed anti-depressants on the first visit to the Dr. Is it just me that thinks this is crazy?

We can change this naturally; science has proven it. We can educate our kids about the challenges that life can and will most likely throw at them and more importantly that it is okay, it's life, these challenges can be overcome. We can teach them that half of the challenges (we think) we face today, would likely be non-existent, if they simply learnt to control how they look at the world and themselves. We can teach them, that it doesn't have to be as tough as we all seem to be making out that it is. We can instil in them the belief and faith that with the right mindset, by choosing to focus on the positives in all situations they are faced with, that they can live happy and fulfilled lives. We can teach that by putting a little effort into all aspects of their life, happiness is possible. We can teach them to focus on and accept themselves, to be happy with who they are, without continuously wanting to compare themselves to others. We can teach that with positive goals and with a vision for the future that they can and will achieve success. Living a life fulfilled, less stressed, less depressed, less anxious, and less negative, is not all that difficult. This is what we should be teaching.

I appreciate that true depression wouldn't allow a person to recognise the positives over the negatives, but if the focus for young people were on the positives from the outset, if we prepared them properly for the challenges that life can sometimes bring and how to overcome them, we might actually see these shocking suicide and depression statistics in young people decrease.

More importantly, we must first implement these teachings ourselves and be an example to the young people of this world!

We live in a world where there is help and there is hope! The people in the images below didn't have the resources and the focus on mental health that we see today. The only comparisons we should be making against others, is how worse off many others are and being grateful for what we do actually have now.

Now that is a BAD DAY.

(Petrified at the thought of going over the trenches into the face of war and almost certain death)

(Still capable of laughing in the toughest of times)

I know my opinions aren't going to go down well, with a lot of people. But as you can tell, I am not okay with not being okay. I am not okay with my loved ones not being okay. It is time for change!

I want to start this book off with a simple challenge. I challenge you, for the next 3 days, to replace any negative thought that might crop up with 3 positive thoughts. It can be 3 things in your life you are grateful for, or just take a second to stop and try to identify the positive in whatever situation is facing you. Really think about it, what are you truly grateful for? What is a positive in your life right now? Each morning (on the 3 days that you choose) I want you to start your day of thinking of 3 things you are grateful for. This must be before your day has even started and lets just see if it makes the slightest bit of difference. What have you got to lose?

Notes:

(Use these blank pages to make notes on the topics and methods discussed in this book... Be creative, draw pictures, do sums maybe working out your budgets, write a shopping list, a to do list, learning from the events of your day. Whatever the case, use the blank pages for you)

3 Things I am Grateful for – Day 1

-
-
-

3 Things I am Grateful for – Day 2

-
-
-

3 Things I am Grateful for – Day 3

-
-
-

 IT IS **NOT** OKAY TO NOT BE OKAY

A note from me to you

No matter where you are in life right now, weather you are at the top of your game or have hit rock bottom there is one thing we have in common. We are all wanting to feel better and to be doing, better! Which is why, weather this book is borrowed or brought, you are reading it right now. You want to feel better or to be doing better in at least one area of your life. You have a vision of the future and that means, I am delighted to tell you, there is hope.

Where we seek answers, advice, or similar experiences we are seeking a way out, or a better way forward. I can tell you from experience, these thoughts can begin to open endless opportunities to **making yourself** feel better. You have not given up, you can succeed, you can achieve, you name it the world is your oyster.

I want to point out the bold text there. Nobody can do this for you, nobody but you! I wouldn't be here without the support of my amazing family and specifically my amazing wife, but it is us as individuals who must make the choice to pick ourselves up, dust ourselves off and create our own future. It is us, it is me and it is you who must make the decision that "it is **NOT** OKAY, to not be OKAY". We can either choose to stay where we are or we can choose, a better way forward and we can do it one day at a time.

"I am no longer cursed by poverty because I took possession of my own mind and that mind has yielded me every material thing I want, and much more than I need. But this power of mind is a universal one, available to the humblest person as it is to the greatest."

Andrew Carnegie

It is said that the law of attraction is a "pseudoscience", a New Thought philosophy but, if you look at the book TNT – It rocks the earth by Claud M Bristol, it was published in 1932 and references everything to do with the application of the law of attraction. There are scriptures dating back thousands of years that talk about the application of the law of attraction. So, I'm not sure about it being called a "New thought Philosophy". Either way, it brings no harm and only good can come of it, so I am all for it. It has helped me, as you will see from my story, and I believe it can help you too.

"The greatest discovery of my generation is that human beings can alter their lives by altering their attitudes of mind. Your mind has the ability to make dreams a reality. It is dependent on you to fully immerse yourself in your mind and explore its creativity"

William James

1842 – 1910

Setting small goals, has been proven to see more success than setting huge, goals. Huge goals with no mini goals or way of measuring progress, are hard to maintain and in turn only make us feel worse about not having achieved them. Often, we remain in that dark hole or fall even deeper. That is not saying you shouldn't set huge goals, do! But, once you know what that huge goal is, it is then you must set about creating those smaller goals, a pathway to that big end goal if you like.

Think of it like a builder building a wall, the end goal is one big solid wall but to achieve that, you must lay one brick at a time.

Small goals are easier and quicker to achieve, the feeling of accomplishment can be felt sooner and more regularly, and this is what will keep you motivated to remain on track.

An example might be you want to save £100 a month! Okay, so how might you break that down to smaller achievable goals? First off, you could work out what your outgoings are (a week) and what you realistically need a week to live off. This should give you an idea of disposable income. In this case you will need to put away £25 a week, for the coming month. If one week, you can only afford £20, that's okay, do you workings out again and you can add £5 to the following weeks savings or extend your target date a little, the important thing is to stay on top of how you are going to achieve your goal. Write it down, create a tracker whatever you do you want to see it, engage with it every day. Measuring or keeping track of the smaller goals allows you to see your progress and it's this that keeps you motivated. You could even break it down to the day, £3.58 per day totals £25.06 a week, £25 x 4 weeks in a month total = £100.

You have achieved your small goals which has led you to achieving your big goal.

I use a similar tracker to this

Start Date:				Amount I want to save:				
By When Date:				My Reason for Saving				

How much I need to save by Day: £

How Much I need to Save by Week: £

Week 1	Monday	Tuesday	Wednesday	Thursday	Friday	Saturday	Sunday	Total Week Savings
£								£

Week 2	Monday	Tuesday	Wednesday	Thursday	Friday	Saturday	Sunday	Total Week Savings
£								£

Week 3	Monday	Tuesday	Wednesday	Thursday	Friday	Saturday	Sunday	Total Week Savings
£								£

Week 4	Monday	Tuesday	Wednesday	Thursday	Friday	Saturday	Sunday	Total Week Savings
£								£

Total Month Savings   £

I'm using money as an example here because let's face it, who doesn't want more of the stuff. The point is this, any goal we are aiming to achieve is made more all the more possible by breaking the goal down into mini goals or milestones where you can track your progress. Be it weight loss, weight gain, an exercise goal, career progression, the list could be endless, the method is simple. Figure out what it is you want and then build your roadmap, your plan, your mini milestones, mini goals on how you intend to get there and then act on it, One day at a time!

Visit our website for downloadable trackers - https://mindset-movement.co.uk/

"I would visualize having directors interested in me and people that I respected saying that "I like your work" or whatever that is. I wrote myself a check for $10,000,000 for acting services rendered. I gave myself 3 years and I dated it Thanksgiving 1995. I put it in my wallet and I kept it there, and it deteriorated... But then, just before Thanksgiving 1995 I found out I was going to make $10,000,000 on Dumb and Dumber."

Make the visualization of your life so strong that it drives you to commit yourself 100% to its development. Hold yourself accountable by imposing a specific timeline to accomplish your vision - this helps you to remain focused.

Jim Carrey

My wife said something to me, not so long ago and it really has stuck. "Don't look at what you can't do, look at what you can do, that you couldn't do a few weeks ago". She reminded me that it isn't about the past, is isn't even about the end goal, it is about the here and the now. It's about achieving all the mini goals or milestones in between and that is exactly where my focus should be applied.

I think some of the literature I have read around the law of attraction can be misinterpreted, well I know it has. "If you believe it, you can achieve it". Like the universe is a magic Genie in a lamp and your wish is its command. True, you must indeed think about what it is you want and if you think about that enough, I believe there is some truth that those thoughts can bring to the light, opportunities that we weren't previously open to seeing. But I do not believe anything is possible on thoughts alone, not without action!

I knew someone once, totally into the law of attraction, read endless books, studied quantum physics, watched endless videos and documentaries on the topic, could tell you everything there was to know. Every year they would say, "this is my year, I'm going to be a millionaire". "I've asked the universe so it's going to happen". Year on year nothing would happen.

JK Rowling, had 12 publishers turn her down before finding success with the Harry Potter books.

Richard Branson started his business out of a phone box. He persisted, he made things happen and it was a student magazine, that he invested in (with a £300 loan from his mother) that sparked the virgin adventure.

According to his high school yearbook, Ralph Lauren's goal was to become a millionaire. At the time, he was living in the Bronx as the youngest child of poor, Jewish immigrants. He enlisted in the Army and worked as a clerk at Brooks Brothers before becoming a business icon. Lauren began his fashion empire with wide neckties (an uncommon fashion trend at the time), and after selling thousands, he launched his Polo line that cemented him firmly into the land of fame and fortune. He even had a cameo on Friends. Today, his estimated net worth is $7 billion. He had a vision and he persisted and made it happen.

Oprah Winfrey is one of the richest self-made women in the world, which is a far cry from her upbringing in rural Mississippi on her grandmother's farm. Winfrey moved a lot. She went from a boarding home in Milwaukee surrounded by extreme poverty and sexual assault to her father's house in Nashville, Tennessee. She dropped out of college early to begin her career in media.

Decades later, Oprah is an entrepreneur legend. Her company, Harpo Productions, is responsible for some massively successful daytime shows, including The Oprah Winfrey Show, Rachel Ray, and Dr. Phil. And an accompanying $2.9 billion dollar net worth isn't too shabby either.

What was the difference between these people, (who by the way all openly practice the law of attraction) and the person I knew, that I mentioned earlier?

They all knew what they wanted to achieve, they all had a Vision, a plan and all were determined, stopping at nothing to achieve it. They acted and were all ready to jump on any opportunity that was presented to them. The difference is, Action!

Thinking, visualising, or meditating on, "I want to lose weight" will not mean you will lose weight. You must think it, you must believe it, you must feel it, how great will it feel? Really see it, keep thinking it.... Tap, tap, tap (More on the tapping later) be inspired by it, and then set the wheels in motion. How are you going to achieve it, write it down? Plan, plan, plan those milestones, set those mini goals, and achieve them, one after the other, one day at a time and you will, I have no doubt, get to the end goal.

Visit our website to download our weight tracker
https://mindset-movement.co.uk/

Chapter 1

7th March 2019, Life was good. No, it was Great!!

I had just got Married to the love of my life, my soulmate. Shortly followed by an amazing honeymoon in Venice, Italy. I was doing well at work, had found a great work and home life balance. I had moved into IT project management which was a change in career direction for me but the direction I wanted to go in for some time and having built a fabulous, loyal, and trusting relationship with my employer, it is a decision they supported and encouraged me in. Everything was great!

I was known as one of those people to not take time off, equally known as one of those people who might be responsible for sharing my cold or sore throat around the office because of it. I would put in hours beyond what I was contracted, was never stressed, or at least never showed it, not enough to ever warrant time off anyway. That's who I was to my team, to my company. Loyal, trustworthy, dependable and someone who went above and beyond.

There I was all grown up with a beautiful family. An amazing stepdaughter, perfect wife, financially sound, roof over our heads, food on the table. No issues other than the normal day to day things that life throws at you, but all in all nothing to complain about. I was happy and looking forward to the future.

I have always had an interest in the law of attraction. Positivity, meditation, visualisation and reading all the books I could possibly cram in. Books that could help me progress personally and professionally. I love to read and follow people's success stories. Always eager to learn and in some way apply the techniques and learnings to my own life.

I would share anything I could in the workplace or with friends, that I felt might be of benefit to them. Always encouraging my team and colleagues to apply the law of attraction in one way or another (although not always so direct as to say, it's the law of attraction because hey that's a load of old rubbish).

When we look at some of the books I mention throughout or the high achiever's success stories that I like to follow, they all apply the law of attraction in one way or another. I would often share success stories to show that anyone can come from nothing. So long as the right techniques are applied and if you are willing to take action to achieve them.

I've talked about Oprah, J.K. Rowling, Morgan freeman, Tony Robbins, Hal Elrod and many others that I know openly apply the law of attraction to their own lives.

By no means was I a millionaire by applying what I was learning *(nor am I now at the time of writing this, but I will be soon)* but a lot of what I had previously applied though, using various law of attraction techniques, had manifested.

Like most people starting out on a similar journey, I dipped in and out and wasn't always consistent with the practices but in my general day to day, I would say I tried to pay attention to what I was thinking, feeling, and putting out there generally.

I saw a future where I would settle down, I saw and visualised having a loving family, a family that appreciated me as much as I did them. I wanted to be doing well at work, I set goals and worked hard to achieve them. I wanted to have food on the table, money in the bank and to not have to struggle financially month to month. I wanted nice holidays, to be able to spend fun times with friends, family and generally to be fit and healthy. All this appeared to be falling into place. I would review previous vision boards that I had made and think wow, that actually happened.

I love fitness, especially boxing and had taken part in quite a few charity fights. This was my vice, boxing, training, boxing, eat, sleep, and repeat! Not that I was the best boxer in the world, I had found the sport in my early thirties but the buzz of training for 8 weeks and walking out to your chosen music, to a big crowd, familiar faces supporting you and shouting your name as you take the long walk to the ring, there was nothing like it.

Adrenalin is a drug and an addictive one at that. One I was happy to be addicted to.

As for the fight itself, anyone who has stepped into the ring will tell you, it goes by so quickly. Trying to recall what happened is almost impossible, I think the adrenalin somehow gets in the way of you feeling any pain or even remembering being punched in the face, until you watch the video back that is.

Just like that it's over and you are celebrating, regardless of if you won or lost. You are celebrating the fact that for the past 8 weeks you dedicated your life to it, your diet, your thoughts and to the hours and hours you spent in the gym.

The whole journey is an achievement, so yes, we celebrate whatever the result, but a win sure does feel good.

I noticed, that the next day and for the week or so that followed, an overwhelming feeling would come over me. A feeling of what now? I wouldn't go so far as to say it was depression but there was something there. There was no end goal. There was no reason to be conscious of what food I was eating, how much water I was taking in, how much sleep I was getting or how many runs or visits to the gym I had made. It was a heavy feeling and probably the first time I realised how important exercise was for my mental health.

For some, fitness comes naturally. My brothers for example could run a marathon without training (That has always frustrated me) I'm not that kind of person, I have to work hard to keep fit and for me it's much easier if there is an end goal.

My bugbear with running is that my brain has a constant intellectual battle with itself. One part is saying "yes run, it's good for you" whilst the other is arguing "why are you running away from the destination you are trying to get back to"? It makes no logical sense! Maybe it was a willpower thing, maybe I was naturally lazy, I don't know but I did better when I had an end goal.

Fitness and its purpose without an end goal, became easier for me when whilst at work one day we were privileged enough to be visited by a key speaker by the name of Jules Mountain. He was a cancer survivor; an Everest avalanche survivor and he had then gone on to summit Mount Everest. *(His last name really is Mountain, he didn't change it to that after the event, I promise).* I won't speak for Jules by telling you his story, it is out there, and I suggest you look it up, the man is an incredible inspiration.

Anyway, he said something during his talk that resonated. Our bodies are much like a vehicle, depending on how well we look after that vehicle, will determine how far that vehicle will take us. Ok makes sense, eat healthy look after ourselves and our bodies will take us further than if we didn't look after ourselves. Simple enough.

Only recently, the MD of the organisation I work for reminded me of this in a motivational speech of his own. "Hypothetically, if a part of your body failed and you were reliant upon a donor organ and you have the choice of these two types of donors, which would you choose"?

Donor 1

30-year-old

Non smoker

Non drinker

Normal body weight for age and size

Zero medical conditions

General Health: Healthy

Donor 2

30-year-old

Smoker 15 years

70 units alcohol per week

Clinically obese

Diabetic

Lung disease

High cholesterol

High blood pressure

General Health: Poor

Easy, you would choose number one, right? He went on, "for most of you, you are not in a position now, where you need a donor. You have a vehicle that is relatively healthy. So, treat that vehicle like number 1. Don't get into a position where you should even have to choose which donor you would prefer. You have a perfectly good vehicle now, look after it".

But the truth is we don't look after ourselves or at least aren't consistent in doing so.

This speech my MD gave prompted me dig out my notes from when we were visited by Jules Mountain. Whilst talking about his own experience of surviving cancer, Jules pointed out to us that from that day forward our bodies were our vehicle, this vehicle is going to carry us for as far and for as long as we allow it. It is the only vehicle we are going to get. Give it the right fuel, keep it active so it doesn't seize up and ensure it gets regular inspections/ MOT's, so that if anything needs replacing it is minor and not major.

The moment he spoke those words, I was on a mission. That was my end goal, to keep this vehicle ticking over and so exercise, diet and general self-care became a lot easier for me. I was feeling great, I had one vehicle and I was going to look after it because I wanted it to carry me as far is it possibly could! I could already see it…. Lindsay Evans lives to 120 years!

"Like Attracts Like. You have to understand: you are a magnet. Whatever you are, that's what you draw to you. If you're negative, you're gonna draw negativity. You positive? You draw positive. You're a kind person? More people are kind to you. ... If you see it in your mind, you can hold it in your hand. This is so true."

You can't think negative and expect a positive life. The life that you want for yourself will be based on the energy that you put out into the universe.

Steve Harvey

Chapter 2

Something that in the past I might have ignored and not visited the Dr for came up, so I went to see my Dr. (Regular MOT's, I remembered Jules Mountain saying)

Something wasn't right, I felt it, my wife felt it and it was affecting my day-to-day life.

There were days I felt like I didn't want to exist. I felt unexplainable anger and what was worse it was for no reason whatsoever. There were days I felt nothing, I cared about nothing, I couldn't sleep but equally didn't want to get out of bed. I wanted to be in the dark, to be left alone. I felt useless and I didn't know what was happening to me. I couldn't concentrate at work. I was snappy with work colleagues and wasn't the person they used to look up to. I didn't have the time or energy for anyone like I did before. I would keep up the pretence to friends and family that I was ok, "yeah everything is fine, just been busy". But they knew!

Having had various tests and visits to the Dr, we found out that I was pre-menopausal, well that explains the mood swings, I can laugh about it now. On top of that, I had some results come back that indicated abnormal cells were present on my cervix. Not a huge concern but concern enough that my GP advised me to go private if I could, to be seen quicker.

I did.

Weeks passed, days at work were missed or I struggled through feeling incredibly unwell. Colleagues were noticing the visible change in my appearance. My colour was off, my face looked gaunt, and I just wasn't my usual self. My office space at the time consisted predominantly of men, so as you can imagine I didn't often talk about my "girl problems". This one day, I remember feeling particularly unwell, I knew I needed to make it out of the office, maybe some fresh air might help. As I had my eyes locked on the door, everything went into a blur and then black!!

"Are you ok Linds?" One of my male colleagues, was standing over me as I came round. "Want me to call an ambulance? you just hit the deck".

"No, I will be fine", I thanked him, got up and made my way outside. I was embarrassed more than anything. I called a taxi and my wife to say I was coming home.

There is no messing around with Katy, *(My wife)*. Hospital it was! She wouldn't have it any other way and there would be no point in getting into an argument that I would surely lose, so off we went.

More tests, some medication and I was sent on my way. Various issues meant that my blood pressure was extremely low, so it was that that had probably caused the faint.

There were more hospital visits, more days of excruciating pain, days that I struggled through work and days I simply couldn't get out of bed to go in, but I won't bore you with the details as this went on for quite some time.

I received a date for my operation.

I was having a hysterectomy, everything that was bad was coming out and I was going to be fine. I could not wait. This had gone on for far too long!

It had got in the way of family life, work life and had got in the way of my own day to day life. Fitness and health plans had gone out the window, the only thing on my mind was the pain. This operation could not come soon enough!

I was sitting in my hospital room waiting for my surgeon to come around and brief me before going to theatre and I remember I was reading one of those magazines *(Take a Break or something like that),* you know the ones where you couldn't make the stories up? How could that even happen to someone, I thought.

I pushed the half-read story aside as my surgeon entered the room. I was feeling generally unwell as I had for a long time but was excited at the prospect it would all be over soon.

As he started briefing me about the surgery, I can remember to this day how he dropped my file and how the papers scattered across the floor. I said, "I hope that's not an omen for how my surgery is going to go" laughing as we picked them up.

A lot of what he was saying was going in one ear and out of the other, I was just so excited that soon I would be feeling better again.

"You will be having a full abdominal hysterectomy" ......
Whoaaah, I'm sorry? What? Why?

All the leaflets and research I had done prior, says that these days especially, keyhole is the preferred option. It reduces the chance of infection, and the recovery time is much quicker than the "old school" full abdominal method.

"Your womb is too big, so its full abdominal" he said.

For anyone wondering, that is a cut from hip to hip, through your abdominal wall in order to remove the womb and cervix.

Katy and I shared a few concerned glances but okay, this guy is a medical professional, Head of Gynaecology in fact, he knows what he is doing, right? and off I went to theatre.

I can't remember waking up in recovery, but apparently, I was asking for my wife so much so that I think I was annoying them. They took me back to my room where my wife had been waiting the many long hours for my return. I remember my parents being there or maybe they joined after, I'm unsure as it's all a bit of a blur.

Suddenly and this wasn't gradual, I felt like my torso had literally been cut in half. A full abdominal hysterectomy *(in other words being cut hip to hip)* felt just like it sounds. Remember, I chose to do boxing for fun, I can get punched in the face with no issues, my pain tolerance is quite high but this, this was something else…. I was dying here! Something was not right!

As I was screaming out in pain, I can remember blurred images of my wife holding my hand and telling me to breathe through it. I could feel my dad's hand holding mine, he was talking to me but not sure what he was saying. I knew something wasn't right for him to be standing by my side, trying to talk me through it. He is the kind of man who would say "get up and run it off" if you broke your ankle. My siblings and I grew up on the football pitch. My dad is an old-school man's man, a tough man and we were brought up that way. My brothers both played for Portsmouth F.C and I for the women's team so, dads efforts paid off. We never went down under a tackle! Well, my brothers might have *(laughs)*.

My mums' distinct northern Irish accent could be heard in the distance, echoing down the corridors. If anyone was going to put this right, she would. I have a vision of her having the nursing staff all in a line against the wall, giving them orders and shouting at them.... That image makes me laugh to this day. I don't actually know if that's what happened exactly, but it was she who noticed exactly what was wrong and went on a rampage to get it sorted. I will stick with the image I have though because it makes me laugh.

It turns out, I wasn't set up with a driver. It's an automated machine that delivers pain relief. According to my chart I hadn't received any pain relief since waking up from my surgery. Every bit of that cut that went straight through my abdominal wall and the site where my womb and cervix had been surgically removed, could be felt literally and it was agony!

I think I even said to my wife, "just kill me". If I had had a gun in that moment, I would have shot myself!

Anyway, my mum had organised the troops (nursing staff) and an hour or so later, they returned with a driver. They set that up and ahhhhh relief! It was heaven, I could relax, I think I just slept.

The next few days were a blur, but I remember on the first night being told to get out of bed so the cleaners could change the bed. I was standing there holding on to my drip trolly just to stay upright. A nurse came in and told them off for getting me out of bed as I wasn't to be out of bed yet, not without a nurse to supervise. I got back into bed, which had to be changed a few hours later as I was lying in a pool of my own blood. They really shouldn't have got me out of bed after all. These things happen, I was alright no real damage done, I thought to myself.

Another memory I have, was when in the middle of the night, I think I rung the nurse buzzer to ask for some more pain relief or something, a dishevelled nurse *(to say the least)* came in. She was clearly unhappy that I had woken her from her sleep and appeared disgusted at the idea of having to go all the way downstairs to get the pain relief, that I required. *(Sorry, lady but I have just been cut in half, is all I was thinking).* She eventually returned with the medication and "kindly" on her way out, moved my table, where my water and my book were along with my TV, out of reach. You know those tv's in hospitals that are on a movable crane arm? I couldn't get much sleep, so my only distraction was either the TV or my book, that was on the table, now out of reach. I dared not press the buzzer again and call her back in.

I wouldn't usually be so timid, but I had no fight in me, none. I was in pain; I was tired, and I was weak.

I cried, on my own, in the dark. I was desperate to be home, desperate to be with my wife, desperate to not feel so alone, I just wanted to feel safe.

It was the next day and a visit from the surgeon, told us everything went as planned and I was eventually allowed to go home. Hurrrrahh. My departing thoughts…. I really think you would get better treatment in a prison and let's not forget; I was paying for the privilege.

I will never forget that car ride home. I felt every stitch, as the car tires that appeared to have lost all contact with any kind of suspension, slowly moved over the road surface. It was as though every tiny bit of gravel was a huge rock. I could tell my wife felt awful, but she couldn't have driven more carefully if she tried.

Finally at home, I climbed into my own bed, and I think for the first time in a long time, I was able to sleep.

Now to get the 6-week recovery out of the way and get back to work, back to fitness and back to my family, just as things were before. I was looking forward to feeling great again. I reminded myself that this pain was only temporary, and every day is a day closer to being back to my old self.

A week in and I already hated being bed ridden, that wasn't me and my wife got the brunt of my feelings. A few more days passed, and I wasn't getting any better. I felt confused, I felt sick, hot and cold. I felt weak.

One morning, I woke, and I could literally ring my top out. I was drenched in sweat. It was a weekend, so Katy organised a visit to the emergency out of hours Dr, something wasn't right.

A few tests later and it was established that I had an infection. My wound was clean, we took great care in ensuring it was, so it must have been an internal infection. "Not to worry, a course of anti-biotics and you should be as right as rain" the Dr reassured.

Thankfully, the antibiotics worked, and I focussed on continuing with my recovery.

Chapter 3

Almost a year had passed, I was expecting by now to have been fully recovered and back to my normal self, but no. Things had gotten drastically worse.

For almost a year I was visiting the Dr every couple of weeks. I was given course after course of anti-biotics and no sooner would they finish, I would have another infection and be back on another course.

I had scans done which identified a compacted infection in my fallopian tube. "Excuse me, what"?

My fallopian tubes were taken during the surgery!

The radiologist confirmed that they most certainly were not, because he was looking right at them on the screen in front of him.

There was also a cyst on my ovary, but nothing to be hugely concerned about. Off I went to wait to hear from the hospital as to what the next steps were.

Then Covid happened.

There were delays with hospital appointments, and rightly so. If the matter wasn't urgent, I agreed that Covid needed our medical professional's full attention. I received a call from the hospital, discharging me as there was no urgency. I had no problem with this, my scans were clear of anything concerning so I needed to get on with it, I thought.

More weeks passed and I was becoming more and more unwell. Something wasn't right, you know, when you know!

I was sleeping more, I was struggling to walk, I had excruciating pain in my hip that shot down my leg. I had zero energy and was looking generally unwell.

The Dr's continued to supply anti-biotics but nothing was helping now.

I felt depressed, I was in a dark hole that I could not get out of, I couldn't be positive about anything. It was the start of the negative flood!

I was useless, I couldn't work, I couldn't do things with my family, I couldn't have fun with my wife and my stepdaughter. I couldn't do things with friends; I was stuck in bed and was useless. For the past year, I had tap, tap, tapped away at myself, telling myself that I was useless, over and over.

I had dark thoughts, and I felt guilty!

My amazing stepdaughter has cerebral palsy and doesn't have use of her legs at all, other than to crawl. My wife was single handily, taking care of her and me. There was nothing I could do to help, nothing. I was useless, a hindrance! So yes, there were times that I thought they would be better off without me.

"Well I mean positively and negatively, I mean you attract, I mean not just what you fear, you attract what you feel, what you are."

What you constantly think is what you produce within your life. If all you see is hopelessness, your life will be a reflection of so. If all you see are opportunities, your life will be full of limitless possibilities.

Denzel Washington

I mentioned earlier that, it is down to us as individuals to make ourselves better. It is a choice and a choice that only we can make. It is us and only us who can choose to move forward but, having a great support network does help.

It can help kick start the action that's required to get you out of that hole, that rut that you are stuck in. Don't be afraid to ask for help. Someone will care and will want to help; you are not alone.

Visit our online community and you will find so many people with stories that are like your own. I can bet every one of the people within the growing community, would be willing to help. Be that by sharing their own stories with you or simply by listening to yours. Most importantly, understand that every one of those people have either come out the other side or are in the process of doing so. It maybe they are still stuck in that rut, but they have chosen a future, not only a future but a positive one. You can move forward too.

Visit - www.mindset-movement.co.uk

Wow! This is my first book; I have always wanted to write but never actually took it very seriously. I didn't know what to write about until now. It is only since my experience and from having an overwhelming feeling of wanting to help other people that, I have been given this opportunity but, how mad is this?

Not so long ago, I was introduced to The Miracle Morning by Hal Elrod.

His book and what has followed has been a game changer for me. Look it up, he has a great story to share.

It's only been in the past month or so that I have set "writing a book" as one of my goals (I haven't shared that information anywhere, other than on a few sticky notes on my goals board in my office, on my vision board and in my own mind. I say my affirmations out loud every morning, per the Miracle Morning guidance but other than that nobody knows)

Well, I have just received an email from the Miracle Morning group that literally reads "Hey Lindsay, quick question for you... would you like to make a significant impact to your income with your own book?" It goes on to explain how I can join a free course delivered by several successful authors on how to write a book and get it published. Now, tell me there isn't something in this law of attraction, positive thinking malarkey!

I can 100% vouch for the fact that since I have chosen my newfound mindset, chosen my preferred state to exist in, opportunities are everywhere.

Anyway, back to the story.

I was in a bad way, enough was enough! Katy had made the decision we were going private, and we were getting this sorted once and for all. I couldn't wait any longer.

This meant more scans and appointments.

"You have a chronic abscess and hematoma, there is a large mass in your pelvice".

My new surgeon showed us the screen and there it was, a huge grey blob that took up most of the picture. There was a visible mass filling the space of where I had my previous surgery. How could that have been missed in my last scan, we thought. With more surgery it could be removed, I would be fine.

My new surgeon was confused as to why I'd had a full abdominal hysterectomy.

"We prefer Keyhole these days".

This rung alarm bells. Thinking back there was no evidence in any of my scans that my womb was too big to be removed laparoscopically. In fact, I remember in one of my previous appointments where we discussed the report of a scan, it mentioned that my womb was "of normal size".

I received the date for my operation.

I wasn't really working now. I was too weak, I could barely move, I was dying I was sure of it! In the final weeks before my operation, I was so ill that even my GP wanted to admit me to hospital. The issue I had was, if I went into hospital, I would have to self-isolate again because of Covid and wouldn't be able to have my operation on the date planned. I physically could not wait any longer and so, I made the decision to hold on and wait.

Those final weeks were tough, the toughest of my life to date.

There was this smell coming from me, from every pore in my body, my skin smelt, my hair smelt, I couldn't get it off me.

I can only describe the smell as "rotting flesh".

It was absolutely disgusting and embarrassing to say the least. I slept for 24 hours straight, my body was exhausted and was giving up.

I hated that my wife had to see me in this way, it was vulgar, and I was on the edge.

Operation day arrived.

I checked in and was excited about the prospects of finally having everything sorted out. I could not go on like this anymore, physically, and mentally, I was done.

My only apprehension about the surgery was my new fear of the surgical theatre. The last guy practically cut me in half for no reason and I woke up having had zero pain relief, so I felt it was justified.

My new surgical team were amazing. They were aware of my previous experience and made me feel as relaxed and comfortable as they possibly could. I was worried about waking up and not having the pain relief I needed, I was petrified of what had happened before. The anaesthetist, knowing my fears showed me her drugs chart, it was already drawn up. I was going to be ok!

When I woke, the only thing that was on my mind was that my wife wasn't there. Understandably, visitors were not allowed because of Covid. Otherwise, it was like staying in a 5-star hotel. They couldn't do enough for me. I wasn't in any pain really, less than before I went in, so that was a relief. The only thing that was uncomfortable was the catheter, but that would be out tomorrow so I could deal with that.

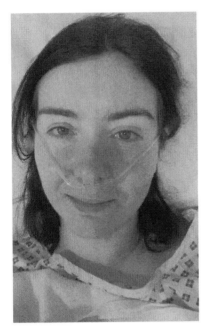

The Fresh from surgery look

Knowing she was likely going mad with worry and would be desperately wanting to see me as much as I her, I video called Katy. I sent a few messages to friends, my parents and to my brothers to let them know I was ok, and I then managed to get some sleep.

This was so far away from my previous experience. I felt looked after and I felt safe.

It was about 7pm when the two surgeons who had operated on me earlier that day came into my room. I could see on their faces that something wasn't quite right. You know when you can just tell that someone has something to say, and you get the feeling it's not going to be good? That's the feeling I had.

I scrunched up my blanket in my hand and squeezed, imagining I was holding my wife's hand.

"Everything went well Lindsay; you are going to be ok". We were able to remove all the infected tissue, the left ovary and both fallopian tubes.

Right, ok that's good. So, why the face, I thought.

Then it came!

"Lindsay, you are extremely lucky, to be alive. What we thought was a chronic abscess was in fact, a surgical swab or surgical material of some sort".

Having never had any surgery before, it had to have been left in since the previous surgery, over a year ago! It was one big ball of infection, they had to remove quite a lot of tissue on the left side to remove it and had to cut my bladder. They explained that I would be needing the catheter for a while, but were hopeful that the bladder would heal, and the catheter could be removed, at some point.

They explained that the smell *(I mentioned earlier)* was because my whole body was septic, I was rotting from the inside, and it was all down to a piece of material being left inside me.

They told me that I wouldn't have survived another two weeks.

The continuous courses of anti-biotics were keeping me from going over the edge, for all that time.

Had Katy not insisted we go private and had she not organised it, I wouldn't be here today to tell this story.

She literally saved my life and every single day when I am scribing what it is that I am grateful for, she comes top of the list.

Just like that, my world was turned upside down, again!

Chapter 4 - The negative flood

I was in shock, none of this should have happened, I shouldn't be here recovering from this second surgery. I shouldn't have been ill for so long, I shouldn't have been made to feel useless' I should've been able to take my dogs for walks, play with my stepdaughter, have fun with my wife, my friends, family, and I should have been able to go to the gym. This was someone's fault, it was not mine, it should not have happened, I felt angry!

The surgeons left the room, and a nurse came in.

"Are you ok"?

You are the talk of the floor; we can't believe what they found during your surgery. It just doesn't happen these days.

For me, that is exactly what I couldn't get my head around. There are still days those thoughts creep up, but they don't help. I know now that those thoughts aren't productive, they only drive you to be even more negative, so I replace them with thoughts of gratitude.

I'm an analyst, my job is to analyse projects, processes, and procedures. So, it comes naturally to me to question how things work and figure out why things happen the way they do. If I knew how it happened, I was convinced it would make me feel better. I mean, I'm no medical professional but weren't there strict procedures and processes in place to make sure this kind of thing doesn't happen? All that consumed my mind was the question, how?

I remember just staring at the wall silently as tears streamed down my face. I should have been focusing on how lucky I was to be alive but all I could think, was how this should never have happened and how I wasn't lucky at all.

The TV was on, but I couldn't hear it. I was in a daze, it's like the world around me had just stopped.

I was in disbelief.

The only other time in my life I felt anything like this was when my nephew passed away, at the age of six.

There is no comparison in experience, God knows I would go through this everyday for the rest of time if doing so could bring him back, but the disbelief I felt in that moment, was similar.

I remember the feeling. Our whole family were together shortly after he passed and I remember a moment when everyone was talking, consoling each other. Everything around me just fell silent. I was staring in pure disbelief over what had just happened, people were talking, I could see their mouths moving but, silence was all I could hear.

Just like that, I came to, I was staring out of the window. I saw a car driving out of the car park, people leaving a house opposite talking and laughing in the street, it felt odd. How could the world still be turning, why hasn't everything just stopped? Our world had just come crashing down around us and nobody knew, nobody cared, people were laughing, the world just continued spinning. I wanted it to stop for a moment, needed it to stop.

"Whatever you hold in your mind on a consistent basis is Exactly what you

will experience in your life"

Tony Robbins

I was angry, I was angry at everything.

Angry at the Gods, at the universe, at the surgeon who did my first operation, at my Dr's who, for the best part of a year prescribed anti-biotic after anti-biotic without realising something was wrong. I was angry at everything that had the power to cause or prevent something like this from happening.

I felt the same way when my nephew passed, I think we all do this at some point in our lives and some more than others.

Why him? Why me?

I have my own thoughts now, on why I think bad things happen to good people and I truly believe that for all the bad things that happen to good people, something good always comes out of it and in some way those experiences end up helping others.

My nephews passing wasn't in vain. He was the reason a charity was set up, providing holidays to families whose children are terminally ill. They get the opportunity, to create precious, everlasting memories. His charity has helped thousands of families, that otherwise would not have been able to afford it.

My experience has led to this book and to building a likeminded community of people who are determined in helping others turn their lives around.

You don't have to look far to see the good that comes from a lot of the bad.

In that moment though, and before all this had become clear to me, I was a state. I needed my wife!

I wiped my face, took a deep breath and I video called her. I'll never forget the feeling I felt when she answered, I could see she was laid back relaxing in the bath. After speaking to me earlier in the day and knowing I was okay, I think it was the first time in a long time that she was able to actually relax. What I was about to tell her, was going to put an end to that relaxation.

"Enjoying a good soak", I asked with a smile.

I was supposed to have called her when my surgeons did their rounds so that she could speak with them, but they came in and it all happened so quickly I didn't get the chance.

"Babe, Mr G and Mr T came to see me". I explained how I was okay, and that surgery went well and that they had got everything out. I then, went on to explain how that huge ball we saw on the scan that day, was a huge ball of infection and right at the centre of it was a surgical swab. "They told me I'm lucky to be alive". She was in shock, at a loss for words.

I tried to make light of the situation by explaining about the catheter and how she will have to go to the toilet for me, literally and we laughed!

We would often Joke when one of us might need to go for a "pee". We would say "whilst you are there go for me, I can't be bothered". The moral of this story is, be careful what you wish for.

Only three times have I ever seen my wife cry; she just isn't the sort. She has been through so much herself; she could write her own book. She's learnt to hold it all back, but on this occasion, she cried! It was more relief that I was ok, I think. The realisation that she was so close to losing me, had hit her.

For the past year we spent so much time going to Dr's appointments, hospital appointments and that whole year we were fobbed off with anti-biotics after anti-biotics.

There was an element of relief in hearing this news because it meant we were right, all along. It was confirmation to us that something in fact was, wrong. It was confirmation that we weren't, going mad.

You expect to be taken seriously by Dr's, you trust that they know what they are doing and for all that time, we felt we were let down.

The past year had put a strain on our relationship, understandably. My wife was having to do everything. Work, take care of the house, our daughter, our dogs, and take care of me all on her own. My parents and Katy's mum were amazing *(I truly have the best mother-in-law),* we would be lost without them, but they weren't there 24/7 and it was all on Katy.

We couldn't do much together, I was always in too much pain, or I had no energy. It was hard on her; I know it was. I couldn't make her feel loved, I couldn't make her feel wanted, I couldn't give her all the things she deserved as my wife and lover. So, I think for her it was also confirmation that it wasn't that there was anything wrong with her. It was confirmation that my feelings towards her had not changed. It was confirmation that there really was something wrong, all along.

She asked if I had spoken to my parents, I hadn't. I was so tired and knowing what their reaction would be what any decent parents' reaction would be I wasn't ready to add fuel to my already burning fire of anger. She said that she would call them to let them know.

I spoke to one of my close friends that evening and that cheered me up. She is always one to make a joke out of anything and not take life too seriously, it helped. My grandad who passed some time ago, was adamant that anything could be overcome with a bit of humour, and I must say that now, I agree.

Katy had told my parents that I didn't want to talk about it right now. I just wanted to focus on my recovery and didn't want any anger to get in the way of that. I received a message from my mum saying that they wouldn't mention it, but if they could have a call before I went off to sleep for the night, they would love that.

I knew they had been worried sick, so I gave them a call. They put on a good act, laughing, and joking. It was comforting to hear their voices. They were just so happy I was ok. I know hearing my voice made them feel better and it made me feel better too.

I have a fantastic relationship with my parents. I am very privileged and grateful for that fact every day. We are very close and being the youngest of their three children I will always be their baby, always have been always will be.

Speaking to my mum that evening helped me put things into perspective for a moment.

"You can't get rid of a bad penny" she would always say. This woman had been through more than you could possibly imagine. Survived cancer several times and only last year barely survived an infection in her spine. She had to learn to walk again after one of her vertebrae completely crumbled due to the infection in her spine. Somehow, she still manages to smile every day and always manages to look on the bright side of life.

She takes each day as it comes, it might be good, it might be bad, but she is grateful to be alive and when she can enjoy herself, she sure will.

The years of treatment and medication has been hard on her. It has affected her body, a lot. Her bones and her health in general have been impacted, but nothing will hold her back. She is the best mum and grandmother anyone could wish for.

If I can be anywhere near the woman my mum is, I will get through this easy, I thought.

My dad's unwavering support, over the years and the way he has dedicated himself to looking after my mum has been inspirational. They truly are the definition of soul mates.

(Mum and Dad posing for the camera)

(Mum learning to walk with her back brace & Dad by her side as always)

It's funny, I never really settled before. No relationship ever matched up to that of my mum and dads, they set an example to look up to and so I simply could not and would not settle for less. I was convinced I would never find it; you don't often see that kind of relationship these days. Until I met Katy, and all those dreams come true.

(Me and Katy)

Chapter 5 - I am not Okay and that is NOT Okay

I was finally home. In bed, unable to move much with the catheter. Katy literally having to wait on me hand and foot, again. Washing me, feeding me, going to the toilet for me, getting my meds and making sure I had enough to drink. Every single bit of independence I had, was gone.

"Make sure you wash your hands". "Make sure you use alcohol wipes on that catheter".

I was using alcohol wipes and sometimes bleach wipes on my own skin. My skin was irritated with the constant cleaning. Inside, I had this overwhelming feeling that everything, had germs. I was becoming obsessive and not only about that.

I was taking my own temperature about five or six times an hour. Just in case.

Last time I got an infection a week or so after my previous op, so I couldn't be too careful, I would tell myself. Besides, it was the only thing I had any control over.

Sleeping in my own bed was nice, but I didn't get much sleep. Whatever way I lay, the catheter would pull.

10 days until my scan to see if my bladder was healing. 10 long days, in bed doing nothing, I wasn't allowed to move. I was bored and frustrated, I'm not one who likes to sit still for too long and I'd already spent most of the past year in bed, I'd had enough of this.

My parents visited and I put on a brave face, even getting up out of bed to show them how well I was.

My friend visited and my brother and his fiancé brought dinner one night. They put chairs in my room, so I could stay in bed but we could still be together and it was nice, chatting and eating and laughing together.

These visits passed some of the time and I will be forever grateful to the people who took the time to visit me. I was overwhelmed with the amount of well wishes I had received. My dressing table was full of flowers, there really were so many people that cared but this feeling only lasted moments.

My room became my safe place. I was going to stay here for ever, I didn't need goals anymore!

Did you know that less than 5% of us stick to our New Year's resolutions? Why is that you wonder.

The new year always seems to be the perfect time to set ourselves a goal, "new year new me" and all that.

The problem most people have and the reason most people fail is because they set a huge goal, and that's it! They decide they want to lose a stone and they go to the gym. Many decide they are only going to eat salad, for the month of January. *(No wonder people give up, salad for a month, no thank you).* Who would want to maintain that? And that, is exactly why, people give up.

There is no variety, no mini goals and nothing to measure progress, so it gets boring. Without being able to measure our success and feel great about achieving those mini goals, we get fed up, forget our reason "why", lose motivation and give up.

The people more likely to succeed are those with a plan. Let's take a weight goal. If you knew that, to achieve your end goal, you needed to lose 3.5 pounds a week, which equates to 0.5 pounds a day, you would see results quicker and each mini goal achieved would give you a constant sense of accomplishment making it more likely you will achieve your overall goal.

It has been proven that being able to see results sooner rather than later, along with a reminder of our reason "why?", is what keeps us inspired and motivated to stick it out and achieve what we set about doing in the first place.

I know for some people they don't like watching the scales every day and in some cases I would advise against this but if you have no medical condition preventing you from doing so then having something to measure and visually see your progress helps. This doesn't just count for weight goals. It might be that you are going to exercise X times a week. It could be you are going to eat healthy food five days of the week. Whatever the case, create a chart so that you can measure and keep track of your progress, your chances of success increase dramatically by doing so.

Visit - www.mindset-movement.co.uk to access our free downloadable trackers which will increase your chances of success.

Sticking at something just means you are creating a new habit. There are so many different views and opinions around how long it takes to make or break a habit, but I go with 30 days, just to be sure.

One of the biggest obstacles preventing most people from implementing and sustaining positive habits is that they don't have the right strategy and they aren't prepared for the emotional aspect it brings. By not knowing what to expect and by being ill prepared to overcome the mental and emotional challenges that are part of the process of implementing any new habit, it makes it more difficult to achieve.

When you are prepared for what the first 30 days are going to bring, by having a plan in place and something you can visibly measure, you are more likely to succeed, fact. When you are prepared, you are more likely to be one of the 5% who do not fail, fact.

Let's break the 30 days down into three 10-day phases.

Whatever it is you are trying to change, weight, exercise, quitting smoking is likely to make you feel like this -

1 – Unbearable

2 – Uncomfortable

3 – Unstoppable

The first few days of any new habit is the most exciting. Its new, you have told yourself you are committed and for the first few days, you go at it with the heart of a lion and with true belief that you are going to do it. But then, the newness wears off and reality sets in. The family are having pizza tonight or friends are meeting at your favourite restaurant for a meal and a few drinks, it's so hard to say, no! Your body and mind resist this new you. Every cell in your body is screaming at you not to do it and so, we slip back into our old ways (admit it, we have all done it).

By knowing that these 10 days are going to be tough and are the "maker or breaker" of you forming this new positive habit, puts you at an advantage, because you know the feelings you are going to experience are temporary and that the reward of achieving your goal is totally worth it, for the sake of 30 days feeling uncomfortable. 30 days in comparison to our entire lives is nothing really, is it?

Will power plays a part, but I now like to use the term "why power". All the successful people out there are using it. It is proven to work. By continually remind ourselves of why, we want to achieve the goal we have set, actually increases the chances of us succeeding. If you do fail, then it is likely that you didn't want it that much in the first place.

For me, I remind myself of my "Why's" every morning. I see them everywhere I look; I've written them. It's on my laptop, on my goals board, in my journal, on my phone, in my mind. It might be worth building "affirmations" into your morning routine too. It really works, I promise.

Repeat to yourself, maybe whilst looking in the mirror when brushing your teeth or maybe whilst you are in the shower (it can be out loud or in your head, whatever is more comfortable for you) "The difficulty I am feeling is temporary, the difficulty I am feeling is temporary, the difficulty I am feeling is temporary….". "I am doing this to feel confident about my own body", "I'm doing this to feel confident in my own body", "I'm doing this to feel comfortable in my own body".

If you are anything like I was, then it's likely you are saying "what a load of old rubbish", right now. But I can guarantee that if you implement this into your daily routine, you will see positive results.

I guarantee that if you stick at it, it will, get easier and soon you will realise that there is nothing preventing you from going for that meal with your friends, you can still remain on track because you will be in a better more determined and disciplined state of mind. You will most likely want, to choose the healthier option, or you might realise that one meal out with friends isn't the end of the world, and that everything is ok in moderation.

"The greatest tool you have in your possession is your mind. Once you take full control of your mind there is no limit to what you can accomplish because you don't allow defeating thoughts to hold you back - you are more willing to take risks."

It's the same process I used in bodybuilding: What you do is create a vision of who you want to be — and then live that picture as if it were already true.

If you are poor, it doesn't mean that you have to live your life in a poor manner. Even if you can't afford material things, if you operate with the mindset and actions of a millionaire, you will produce a millionaire lifestyle.

Arnold Schwarzenegger

Chapter 6 – When you don't practice what you preach

Katy, continued to look after me, I continued to have visitors and I continued to lay in bed. I didn't need to get out! Every few hours, Katy would take my catheter bag and go to the toilet for me, literally no reason to get out of bed. My excuse was, "I'm recovering".

My room was safe, it was clean, and I was being looked after. Those habits I spoke of creating earlier, can also be bad ones. Physically, I was recovering. Mentally I was going backwards, day by day, creating some very bad habits.

Rarely did I have to leave my room, so I didn't. I noticed that when I did, my palms would become sweaty, my heart would race, breathing rate would increase and I felt dizzy and nauseous. That's my body alerting me to the fact that stepping outside of my "safe zone" was not a nice feeling, it wasn't safe, so I had best stay in my room, I told myself.

I had a lot of time to think, most of my thoughts were around how this happened and who was at fault. I had angry thoughts, depressed thoughts, thoughts that I was useless. I had convinced myself that I was and so I acted like it. My brain was in a constant supply of cortisol there and so, was getting everything, it needed.

Before my operation I had pain pretty much everywhere. That pain was gone now but I still had this pain that ran down my left thigh, from my hip. What was that? I had a lot of time to think of the pain and fuzzy sensation in my leg. I thought about it so much so that it even began to consume me in my sleep!

I started to have nightmares. I was on a trolley being wheeled down a hospital corridor. The panel lights in the ceiling flashing past as I was being wheeled somewhere. When I looked down towards the foot of the bed, it was the Surgeon. Pulling me towards double doors that had a bold red, flashing sign that read THEATER. Paralysed and only able to move my head I look back and I see Katy trying to pull me backwards in the other direction. BANG, we would hit the theatre doors and I would wake, with a start. Absolutely dripping in sweat.

I must have an infection; I would grab the digital thermometer and check immediately. This nightmare would recur over and over and over, every single night.

I would find myself watching TV until 2 or 3am, just to avoid going to sleep, to prevent myself from experiencing that nightmare again. Eventually my body would give in to tiredness and there I was, in the same corridor.

On the odd occasion when for whatever reason the pain in my leg would flare up, I would dream that I wake up on the operating table, just as the surgeon was cutting my leg off. I'm no psychologist or dream expert but I gathered the thoughts I was having daily, paired with the pain in my leg was subconsciously causing these dramatic "dream scenes". I had become obsessive, and I needed to do something.

I spoke with my GP about the pain in my leg, the OCD, and the trouble I was having sleeping. He gave me more painkillers, pills that would help me sleep and referred me to OCD group counselling.

I tried the group counselling but to be honest, I'm not a talker and especially in a group environment. I never have been and whist I knew these obsessive thoughts were a form of OCD, to me, I was different. By no means am I saying the experiences of the other people were any less than mine, but it was different. I hadn't always had this. I knew that what was happening to me then in that moment, was related to my experience of recurring infection. My constant use of the thermometer was a control mechanism related to that. These people had no obvious reason for what they were doing, they needed something different to me. I just needed help in breaking my thought patterns that were directly related to an individual experience, so I didn't go again.

With my bladder healing extremely well, my catheter was removed just after the 10 days. The recovery (this time) was just over 8 weeks in total. I was able to get up and about a bit more easily. I had the same sweaty palms and could literally hear my blood pumping through my veins but generally if I was with Katy, I felt safe. She saved my life, she looked after me and she along with my bedroom became my safe place!

I noticed if anyone asked me to do anything, if it meant being without Katy, I would find and excuse not to do it.

I wasn't safe without her, what if I got ill? What if something happened... nobody would recognise the signs but her. It's too risky, I told myself.

I had to use crutches to get about as my leg was too painful and would often give way. We went on walks with my parents or would take the dogs for a walk to the park. I was reliant on a wheelchair for anything more than a few hundred yards. I absolutely hated this; I went from exercising five days a week to not being able to walk without aid.

In a follow up appointment with my most recent surgeon, he said the leg pain and sensation was likely nerve damage due to the infected material being sat there for so long, eating away at my soft tissue and so he referred me to physio. Again, we were reminded of just how dumb struck he and the other surgeon were whilst performing surgery. He actually said, "we looked at each other and were like, what the fuck is this". You had every reason to be feeling as poorly as you were Lindsay. He recommended and prescribed a new pill for the nerve pain in my leg and felt confident that it might help with my sleep too.

It didn't really do much for my sleep, neither did it do much for my nerve pain but thought best to stick with it, it might take a while.

Now I was running on little sleep, fear of infection had gotten worse, nightmares had gotten worse, and I had just about had enough. Whilst I could talk to katy about anything there is always a certain amount you hold back. I didn't want to burden her anymore; I didn't want to let her down…. Every day she would tell me how proud of me she was, proud of my progression. I didn't want to let her down. I didn't want to speak to my mum, how could I be complaining after what she has been through.

The truth is, I was feeling much better health wise but because of the physical impact and the emotional impact, mentally I was not feeling good at all. In the past, I would go out for a run or go to the gym and take my feelings out on the punch bags. I couldn't do any of that.

I would look at my amazing stepdaughter, who doesn't have use of either leg, who is entirely reliant on a wheelchair to get around and she would manage day in day out, without complaining. I would look at her and think what a failure I am. I still had my life, my newfound health and yeah I struggle on the one leg, but I can at least take myself to the toilet.

No matter how much I told myself that, I still felt sorry for myself. I would look at my mum who's only thoughts right now were of me. She wanted me to be alright, she would say in disbelief "I can't get over what you have been through Lindsay" All the while I'm thinking God mum you are a medical miracle, you have been through so much and yet you are still able to smile, still able to put others before yourself and I'm sat here feeling sorry for myself. No matter how hard I tried, I could not get out of that mindset. I beat myself up, day after day, after day and I had chosen to stay sat in it!

I decided to act, enough was enough!

My scheduled physio appointment was a while off, too long for me to wait, so I found my own physio.

I knew that I needed someone outside of my family and friends to talk to, so I found a councillor.

"Constantly remind yourself of the person you are destined to become - it develops the mindset and actions that guide your life. Before you realize it, the mindset and the actions you implemented will produce the results you desire".

Lady Gaga

Chapter 7 - Tap, tap, tap! Repetition is key

With any habit, good or bad, repetition is key!

Take smoking for example, the first cigarette you put to your lips and that first inhale, is not an enjoyable experience. I challenge anyone to find me someone who would say otherwise. It is the repetition that creates the habit.

You may have heard of the old torture method of dripping water on a forehead, or you may be familiar with "Kipling's boots"? It was the continuous, never-ending stomping of the boots that made men mad. The Repetition. You see, it can work in both ways, good and bad.

It's the repetition of anything that makes its mark on the human mind. We see it in modern day advertising.

We have seen it recently on the news with the Covid statistics. Continually in our face, over and over to ensure we are all fully aware of the severity and to remind us to be fearful of what's out there. Tap, Tap, Tap!

The difference between the subconscious and conscious mind are close. If you can get a definitive detailed picture in your conscious mind by using the process of repetition and make the subconscious mind, click, you have at your command a power that astounds. If only we knew what we wanted, with the act of repetition we could achieve pretty much anything.

Often, the challenge we face in today's world is, we don't know exactly what it is that we want. With so much choice and with such busy lives, it's difficult to really find the time to stop and to understand what it is that we truly want.

We are followers, we do things because "it's just what everybody else is doing". A recent study showed that 94% of retired people, who had been in the same job for 20 years or more had not been happy and retired not feeling, fulfilled. When asked why they went to work, day in day out to a job they did not enjoy. The majority answered with something like the following - "because everyone goes to work, you just have to". "Nobody enjoys work, It's just, life".

We could describe ourselves and life today, like a rubber ring being carried on a fast paced rapid.

To repeatedly focus on what we want and to take the action necessary and required to achieving or obtaining what we want, we must stop for a moment.

The first thing we need, is to understand what it is we want and ask ourselves why we want it. Once we understand and can truly believe and feel our "why" the spirit and desire to get what we want, will flow.

For me, meditation has helped me do that. Meditation has been that stop, in the rapid. As I mentioned earlier, I practice the teachings from The Miracle Morning by Hal Elrod. I apply the SAVERS exercises, every morning. Meditation being one of the exercises helped me find some quiet time, time to quiet my brain and get a better understanding of what it was, I wanted. Once I repeated that and had a clear vision in my mind, I wrote down what it was, that I wanted. I created affirmations in relation to the things I wanted and every morning (sometimes more than just morning) I work through the techniques Hal Elrod talks about.

Silence, Affirmations, visualisation, Exercise, Reading and Scribing.

It's simple.

You spend 1 hour a day, in the morning (10 minutes on each exercise) repeating the same process everyday over and over, Tap, Tap, Tap.

Once you know what you want and have your list of affirmations, it is beneficial to see visual images of the things you want. I created a power point for each area of my life I want to improve. Things like, relationships, career, fitness, health, weight, income, goals (such as writing this book).

Some people like to create vision boards and hang them up in their office. Printing and sticking pictures to it as they go. Some people like to create a catalogue with a new note pad or might stick pictures in a journal. Do whatever works for you but being able to see exactly what you want often and visually helps tap into that subconscious. I look at my vision board every morning as I am preparing for my day at work.

Next comes exercise, now this doesn't have to be strenuous. Hell, I had given up all hope of ever being able to exercise again and I'm doing it. There are no excuses, you can sit in your chair and do armchair yoga. You can google armchair exercise and in seconds see a video with guidance on how to exercise from your chair.

If, however, you are able. Get out and go for a brisk walk, or jog on the spot, anything to get your blood pumping and those endorphins flowing. There is nothing better, than to start your day with a bit of exercise and remember it's not hours in the gym that's needed, each practice is 10 minutes long. Anyone can do it …. No excuses!

Next comes reading.

For 10 minutes, read a book that is going to empower and inspire you. A book that is going to benefit you in some way! It might be business related, are you wanting to start a new business? It might be fitness related or nutrition related. It could be you are interested in starting a new hobby or to become better at saving Money? It really could be anything, just ensure whatever it is, it is going to help you on this new journey and that you will be able to learn from it.

Some people prefer to do this part in the car on the way to work listening to an audible. Whatever suits you, do it.

The point is that you are in a state of constant, uninterrupted learning for this 10-minute period, every day.

Finally, 10 minutes of scribing, or journaling if you would prefer. For 10 minutes write about, what it is you are grateful for on this day. What you might have learnt this week from your readings, what you are doing to achieve your goals. You can look back on these inserts later and see how far you have come or use them as a reminder of where you intend to be going.

All these practices are positive, all of them will benefit you in some way and all of them is more than what you were doing before, and the best bit about it is, it only takes sixty minutes of your day, sixty minutes to change your life for the better.

What are you waiting for? If you are sick and tired of being sick and tired, then start today. I promise you that if you put the effort in, it will change your life!

I really don't want to steal any of Hal Elrod's thunder, and I have barely touched the surface of his book so please do purchase The Miracle Morning by Hal Elrod, it is available on amazon and in good bookstores.

The reason it is called the miracle morning is because it is intended to be done in the morning, before your usual day kicks off. If you usually wake up at 7am, wake up at 6am if you usually wake up at 8am wake up at 7am, It's simple, that's how you find that hour to do it. It is all too easy to say "I haven't got the time" or "I'm just too busy" which is, I am sure what a lot of you reading this are thinking. Yes, we are all too busy to be fitting this in throughout the day or even worse at the end of the day when we are tired and just needing to relax. I need that extra hour sleep, I hear you say.

Starting your day in this way, really sets you up for the day ahead and when you realise how good it makes you feel, how positive and how full of energy you become and how ready you feel for the day ahead, you won't mind losing that hour in bed. Hey, you might even end up doing it at weekends too!

Waking up early on a Saturday gives me an edge in finishing my work

With a very relaxed state of mind. There is a feeling of time pressure on weekdays that aren't there at weekends. If I wake up early in the morning, before anybody else I can plan the day or at least my activities with a relaxed mind.

Oprah Winfrey

I had repeatedly told myself I was in danger of getting an infection. No matter how many times I told myself that everything, I was now fearful of such as, having a bath, going swimming, laying in bedding that was more than a day old was not responsible for my previous infections, it didn't matter.

I had tapped, tapped, and tapped enough to convince my brain that I was in danger and then my brain went to work as, it was designed to do to alert me of every danger there was around me. I had done the same with my thoughts around leaving the house without Katy. I had probably done the same regarding my thoughts to do with my physical capabilities. I had implemented the wrong mindset, in every area I could.

It is also important to mention that we must also be aware of what we are paying attention to and receiving from external sources.

Every physio and similar therapist I saw were telling me, this is life changing, you are going to have problems with this leg for life and if not life its years we are looking at here Lindsay. They told me not to do this, not to do that. Tap, tap, tap. I heard it, processed it, focussed on it, I trusted those sources and so come to believe it, it got me down.

Deep inside, I knew I was capable of more. I knew, I had to change this mindset to start making progress and so I started to study, the how!

"I am not what happened to me, I am what I choose to become"

Carl Jung

The organisation I work for were doing a challenge for charity. The goal was to walk or run the distance between our offices and Africa. By combining the miles, we achieved individually would be how we reached the overall target. There were some incredible efforts. One guy completed the equivalent of 5 marathons in one weekend, I think it was and another a good friend of mine came not far from doing the same.

I wanted to take part, I want to walk one of those miles, I decided!

Supported by my good friends and colleagues (my wheelchair on standby) I walked with crutches 1 mile. It took me an hour and a bit to complete, but I did it.

For me, that was as challenging as 5 marathons in one weekend, it was tough but at no point was I getting in that wheelchair. I would have crawled if I had to. I felt great!

The next day reminded me that it was indeed like running 5 marathons, I felt PAIN!

I had an appointment scheduled with my physio who had already told me not to do it, but she probably knew I was going to do it anyway, being a friend of the family and knowing what we were all like.

It was a tough session; one I remember to this day and won't forget for a while! Having been on a high about the whole ordeal, I came down with a huge thud.

A mile, something I once would have easily been able to run, in fact it would have been a warmup in boxing camp was literally the hardest thing I have done physically in my life. The pain it caused was unbearable and again, my thoughts caused me to sink inwards mentally.

I spoke at lengths with my councillor about how it made me feel. About, how it's not me to get depressed so easily, how it was so difficult to let go of what I could do in the past and can't do now and how it was so hard to remain positive all the time.

I'm no therapist but I picked up on a pattern that she would use on me during most sessions. She would say "if your best friend were you in this moment right now, what would you say to them"?

She would continually remind me, every time I discussed a feeling or emotion that it was normal to feel that way. She would remind me of what I had been through over the past couple of years and ask me if it was someone else, who had gone through it (let's take Katy for example) would I be so critical? Of course, I wouldn't, but I'm not them, I'm me, I know me, and this isn't me.

It is common for us to have higher expectations of ourselves than of others.

We discussed my newly diagnosed, PTSD, OCD and the 5 stages of grief (denial, anger, bargaining, depression, and acceptance). These can chop and change but we kind of worked out that I was in the depression stage. I had been through the stage of not feeling like this had happened to me, that this felt like it was some story in the magazine I had read that day, in the hospital. Everything that had happened over the past couple of years really didn't seem real, at one point. It really didn't feel like it had happened to me.

The point is, for me all I was hearing was how bad everything was. I was being reassured that it was okay to feel this way and I didn't want that anymore. I wanted someone to give me a kick up the butt and say pick yourself up and dust yourself off now.

I knew what I had to do.

 All that was left was acceptance, I needed to accept this. This was very real, it did happen to me, anger will not help, it will not change anything. Life wasn't meant to be lived backwards only forward and that is the direction I'm choosing to head.

We are going forward regardless, time doesn't stand still, Life goes on and the world will continue spinning. One thing is for sure, it will not wait for any of us.

The time is NOW to make the decision. Are you going to change your mindset, for the better?

Visit our website and start the journey –

https://mindset-movement.co.uk/

I made the decision, in that moment and have not spoken to my councillor since.

She was no longer a requirement.

It is my belief that mindset and attitude really does impact what you manifest, what you attract into your life. I had changed my mindset.

I have wobbles and that's ok, but I am focused on recognising when I do. I allow the thoughts or feelings to come in, I acknowledge they are there and then importantly, I let them go. If they are negative thoughts, I put effort into noticing and then replacing with 3 positives and over time I am noticing I'm having more positive thoughts than negative. I'm tipping that balance that I talked about at the beginning of this book. Like anything, it takes practice and consistency.

There are some great guided meditations that are perfect for mastering this if you have trouble in letting go of negative thoughts, a simple google search or YouTube search will find you plenty.

I was seeing a future again and with positive visualisation and by implementing just a few positive practices into my daily routine, it has started opening doors. I started to be and still am being presented with opportunities.

My mind is clear, and I am feeling great.

I visited my parents one day and by chance my brother was there visiting my dad. He was there with his physio and pain management specialist who had treated an old shoulder injury of my brothers and my brother, swore by him.

Lee is a plasterer by trade and having visited several physios and having been told by various medical professionals that he wouldn't be able to use that shoulder again, not properly, he went to Ahmed. My brother is currently in Scotland working on a huge building project and he is plastering to his heart's content, with no issues. None other than old age of course. *(I am aware to expect full payback for this comment Lee)*

Lee convinced me to allow Ahmed to see me, just for 20 minutes. What was there to lose?

I spent closer to 45 minutes with Ahmed.

Going in, I was reliant on crutches and was unable to straighten my left leg. I walked out, without crutches and was able to straighten my leg. There was work to be done, this wasn't going to be fixed overnight but he is the first person who hasn't told me how much this is going to affect me.

He hasn't told me this is for life and in fact he guaranteed me that if I worked with him and not against him that I would see 75% improvement in my mobility inside 12 weeks. The difference this makes to how you feel and think, is incredible.

Remember, what we choose to hear, read, and absorb from external sources, what we choose to plant in our brains from can be just as powerful as what we choose to think about ourselves.

As well as being my physio and pain management consultant. Ahmed has become a good friend.

I am improving week on week and my pain, is managed by me. Almost instantly, I recognised that we had the same outlook. He has not once told me "Not to do" something, in fact encourages me to go do it. He tells me to trust my body, that it will tell me when enough is enough. If I overdo it, I will know about it the next day and will know what not to do next time, besides it's his job to manage my pain and pick up the pieces if I want to enjoy myself.

If I want to push myself by doing something I enjoy then I can. It's like I have been tied up in chains and he had the key to the padlock, to my freedom, to joy and to hope.

I'm excited again!

This man was like a breath of fresh air, he didn't restrict me. He has made me look at pain in a different way, for example I control it, it does not control me. Weirdly, it seems more manageable when I know I have inflicted it on myself doing something I enjoy!

I'm aware that not only is he treating me physically, but he is treating me mentally as well. He uses psychological techniques throughout his sessions that over time has built my confidence and because of him I am back in the gym, I am walking without crutches, I am trusting my leg to hold my weight on its own. I am conscious of when not to, but overall, the improvement has been miraculous.

I'm not a robot, there are times I look around at people running on a treadmill or sparing in the boxing ring, hitting the bags and it hits me. "I want to be doing that, I could do that once!". It's in those moments that I remind myself, it's not about what I can't do now, it's about what I can do, that I couldn't do a week ago.

It's about getting excited for the next few weeks ahead. Knowing I will be doing more then, than I can today. It's about being in the moment and not looking back, only looking forward. Setting small goals and achieving them week on week, one day at a time and celebrating those achievements.

I am achieving more now, than ever!

Only a few days after meeting Ahmed, I was at work. A colleague of mine, who has carved out an unbelievably successful life in all aspects, recommended the Miracle morning and it seemed to come at the exactly right time for me.

The Author Hal talks of a life changing experience that he went through and how he came out the other side and it simply resonated.

Now here I am writing my own book, with a mission to positively impact as many other lives as possible. People who just need that little bit of guidance to find their own way forward.

Claud M Bristol would say "Tell No one of your plans for success".

People, often those closest to us, will try to put you down. Some people will not be happy to see the change in you, they may feel they are being left behind, they may not want to change and join you on your journey.

Some people are threatened by the success of others, and many will simply put you down, out of pure jealousy.

Take this advice. Should barriers accidentally fall or be placed in your path, do not give up!

Climb over or go round those barriers and remember nothing can stop you, but yourself.

My experience isn't the worst thing ever to happen to someone, but it is my own. It is an experience that turned my life upside down and took me to a very dark place. All our experiences are different, no one person's experience is any less or more damaging than another's. Our experiences are our own and it is completely normal to feel however or whatever we feel about our own challenges in the moment.

Don't allow yourself to compare your feelings to others and don't allow yourself to feel judged. Try not to compare how someone else might have handled something similar to what you are going through, you are not them and they are not you. I will say it again because it is hugely important and a huge lesson I had to learn. Our experiences are our own!

Only one thing makes our experiences and how we handle them similar, one thing is true! No matter what the experience, no matter how deep the hole you might find yourself in, if YOU choose to, you can get out. Not only can you get out, but you can excel, succeed, and achieve. Happiness is a choice and one that you, are in control of.

I still have a long journey ahead and I am accepting of that, I'm still adapting to life as it is now, and I will continue to find adaptions that work for me, because nothing is going to stop me.

My story hasn't been told in search of sympathy, I have shared it to act as an example to anyone in a dark place that they are not alone and can move forward and achieve a sense of fulfilment.

Whilst my journey has been tough, it has been the cause of me settling for nothing less than achieving the success I have meticulously planned out and am deserving of.

It is an experience that in the end, I am grateful for.

"Acknowledging the good you already have in your life

Is the foundation for all abundance"

Eckhart Toll

The End

Authors Note

I really hope you enjoyed this book and I look forward to you joining us on our journey to the next one.

Don't forget our mission, to positively impact as many lives as possible, one day at a time.

You can join our community by visiting our website (www.mindset-movement.co.uk) and clicking the Facebook link.

It is a place where you can share your own story. Share the positive techniques you applied that helped you get out of the place you were in.

Sharing your story might give someone else hope and the guidance they need right now. Your story might be the one to inspire someone else to do the same.

It might be, that right now you are in a dark place and just seeking inspiration from others. Whatever the case may be, you will be welcomed to join us and will be a valued member of our ever-growing community.

"Take the first step in faith. You don't have to see the whole staircase,

just take the first step"

Martin Luther King

Next Book

With permission, I will be compiling the stories shared by the members of The Mindset Movement Community and together we will use those stories to create a new book.

The book will be one that we hope reaches further than our community alone and one that helps to positively impact and improve the lives of others.

No longer is it "OK to NOT be OK".

Together we can change this mindset and together we will.

Printed in Great Britain
by Amazon